MW01658285

Bird Sounds

Mick Manning

Houghton Mifflin Harcourt.

Bird Sounds was originally published in English in 2016. This edition is published by arrangement with Oxford University Press.

Printed in China

ISBN 978-0-358-26222-0

1 2 3 4 5 6 7 8 9 10 XXXX 28 27 26 25 24 23 22 21 20 19

Inside cover notes written by Catherine Baker

Acknowledgments

Series Editor: Nikki Gamble

Houghton Mifflin Harcourt Publishing Company
125 High Street
Boston, MA 02110
www.hmhco.com

Contents

Loon

Birds make all sorts of sounds. Some birds sing songs and other birds just make loud noises!

This bird is calling across a lake.

The loon is also called a "diver."
Loons live in many parts of the world.

Mallard Duck

This mother duck calls to her ducklings.

Mallard ducks have about 12 fluffy ducklings.

Tawny Owl

Some owls hoot! One tawny owl calls "Too-wit," then another replies "Hoo-hoo."

Tawny owls are nocturnal. This means they sleep in the day and are awake at night.

Barking Owl

Not all owls hoot.
This owl sounds sort
of like a dog barking.

Barking owls live in Australia. They eat mice, birds, and even rabbits.

Goose

These birds call out as they fly.

Geese need to keep together when they fly. When they call out, it helps them to find each other.

Falcon

This falcon is calling to scare away a crow from her nest.

Falcons nest on cliffs. They also nest on tall buildings in some cities.

Keck-keck-keck!

Cuckoo

This **male** cuckoo is singing to **attract** a **female**. Only male cuckoos sing this sort of song.

Female cuckoos lay their eggs in other birds' nests. This tricks the other birds into looking after the cuckoo's eggs.

Kookaburra

The kookaburra is a noisy bird. Its song sounds like someone laughing!

Kookaburras live in Australia. They eat lizards, mice, and small birds.

Yellowhammer

This bird sings in a pattern that can sound like words.

A little bit of bread and no cheese!

Yellowhammers lay eggs that have wonderful patterns. Each egg is different.

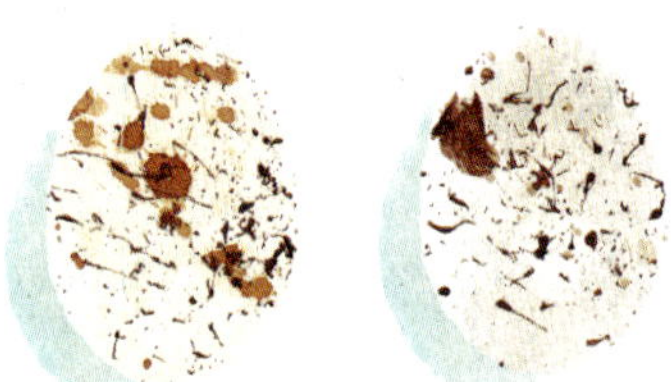

Lyrebird

This bird can copy the sounds it hears.

Lyrebirds live in the **rainforest**. Sometimes people cut down the trees using **chainsaws**. The lyrebirds can copy the sound of the chainsaws.

Glossary

attract: to interest another bird

chainsaws: a saw with a motor for cutting down trees

female: girl

male: boy

rainforest: a tropical forest where it rains a lot

Index